The BLITZ

The BLITZ

WARTIME MEMORIES OF THE LONDON BOMBARDMENT

MARY HANWAY

canary
press

Dependable

Thanks chiefly to their unique gas-tight construction,* Champion Sparking Plugs are ensuring utmost engine-efficiency with economy, and worthily contributing dependable ignition so essential to all motorised units.

CHAMPION SPARKING PLUGS

CHAMPION SPARKING PLUG COMPANY LIMITED

SEALED WITH SILLMENT
★
Champion Plugs are Sillment-sealed against the troublesome leakage common to ordinary plugs. This 'miracle mineral' corrects rough, uneven and wasteful engine-operation caused by using leaky, over-heated sparking plugs.

CONTENTS

THE WAY IT WAS

MY name is Mary Hanway, and I lived at number 11 Pitt Street, which lay just off the Bethnal Green Road in the East End of London. It was a modest, terraced dwelling which housed myself, my older sister Ellen and my parents. On this particular night mother had drawn the black-out curtains and the three of us (father was fighting fires) were huddled underneath the dining room table as the sirens wailed, warning of an impending attack by the Germans. This was the beginning of the period known as the Blitz.

It all started on the afternoon of 7 September 1940, the date when Hitler turned his attentions to the streets of London. Over 300 bomber planes bombarded London for more than two hours, causing major panic as residents ran for shelter, totally unprepared for what was taking place. As a young girl of eleven, that first attack was not only terrifying it also left me feeling a little shell-shocked and uncertain of what was happening.

It always seemed worse at night and the Germans mostly came after dark. As soon as it was dusk, the street lights went out and people

ABOVE: St Paul's Cathedral stands proud amidst the surrounding smoke and fires, barely touched by the Germans' efforts to burn the City of London to the ground.

had to cover their windows so that enemy planes could not use the lights to navigate by, or indeed as targets. I remember the heavy feeling in the pit of my stomach as London prepared for the next attack. Wrapped up in a blanket, under the table, I could feel the vibration on the floor as the heavy bombs did their best to tear the city apart. Mother didn't cry anymore – not like the night of the first attack – she just sat white-faced as she held us in her arms.

As the bombs continued to thud, everything in the house shuddered and you could hear the tinkle of glass from the cabinet in the corner. Then we heard the drip, drip, drip of water falling on the tabletop. Mother let out a gasp and told us to stay there while she went to see what had happened. We pleaded with her not to leave us, but she promised she would be back within minutes. As mother left the safety of the table, I bravely crawled out of my blanket and crept after her in the dark. She climbed the stairs careful not to trip on the threadbare rug on the top landing, using only torchlight to guide her. She opened each bedroom door and peered inside, but it wasn't until she got to my room that she found the cause of the dripping. On my washstand stood a large jug and washbasin which I had just filled with water before the sirens sounded. The jug was intact, but the washbasin had a large crack and a piece missing out of one side. I could actually hear the relief in my mother's sigh as she realised that it was nothing serious.

After three hours everything went quiet and we were allowed to return to our bedrooms. I asked if I could share Ellen's bed as I didn't want

ABOVE: A poster warning civilians to take various precautions to protect themselves against enemy air raids before going to bed.

to be left alone, and as soon as we got into her room we peered through the blackout curtains to see what had happened in our street.

The sight that met my eyes is still vivid in my memory today. The sky was glowing red and we could see much of London was on fire. Out of the smoke loomed an enormous dome, standing proud among the wreckage – it was St Paul's Cathedral, miraculously untouched by the bombs.

On our street, several men wearing tin hats were estimating the damage; everything was covered in dust. I could hear shouting from somewhere in the distance and then something caught my eye. In

ABOVE: Some blackout curtains were fitted with ventilators to allow air circulation from an open window.

The bus we used to take to school had nose-dived into a bomb crater, during one of the first air raids on the East End.

the window opposite, my schoolfriend, Tommy Ward, had his face glued to the glass and was waving frantically to catch my attention. I waved back, but Ellen pulled me away from the window and said that we ought to get some sleep. It took us a long time to fall asleep that night and I remember having vivid dreams that woke me with a start in the early hours of dawn.

It was childhood curiosity that made me want to see the destruction. Along with Tommy and three other friends, we walked the streets of Bethnal Green, having first been made to put on our tin helmets in case something fell on our heads. The first thing to hit us was the choking smell of dust and smoke and a strange odour like cabbage cooking, which turned out to be leaking gas pipes. Of course we should have been wearing our gas masks, but in our hurry to see what had happened that night we had left them behind. We spent much of that morning dodging ARP wardens, because we knew we would be severely reprimanded.

We stood and watched for a while as firefighters fought to subdue the flames of the many buildings that had caught fire that night. Others were frantically searching the rubble in case anyone was trapped. As we turned the corner we were stopped in our tracks. A bus, the

ABOVE: After hearing a faint moaning noise, a dog is used to help rescuers search the rubble.

one we usually caught to school, had nose-dived into a bomb crater; it was an eerie sight. We were quickly ushered away from the area and told to go somewhere safe by the wardens, obviously far too occupied to notice that we were not appropriately dressed.

We weren't quite ready to give up our adventure, so we quickly ran out of sight of the warden and headed off to another area. Most of the streets in our district showed evidence of the night of destruction. We turned round as we heard a dog howling at the end of the road. It was covered in dust, with blood dripping from a wound on its ear, but the most disturbing thing to us children, was the fact that it was glued to the spot, staring at the rubble. Tommy ran back to tell one of the wardens that he believed someone was buried under the debris in the next street. The warden cupped his hands together and shouted for some assistance from any firemen that could be spared. One grabbed a spade, the warden grabbed a huge piece of wood that was lying in the road and the third a makeshift stretcher which, no doubt, he hoped he wouldn't have to use. As they approached the site, the dog whined

pitifully and started scratching at a pile of bricks. The three men dug furiously and told one of us to go and get an ambulance as the warden said he had heard a faint voice. The oldest of our group, Billy Travers, ran off to get help while the rest of us stood mesmerised, a little afraid of what the rescuers were going to find. It was the victim's lucky day, however, apart from being covered in white dust and a nasty gash on his head, the rescuers managed to pull an elderly man from his temporary grave. I don't think I have ever seen anyone so grateful; and his dog, who was visibly excited, wagged his tail and licked his owner all over his face. I imagine the poor man believed his world had come to an end. There were many others, some not so lucky, who were pulled out of the wreckage of the East End, but that was the only one we witnessed.

We headed back to the relative normality of Pitt Street where Susie and I played hopscotch, while the boys played war games. Ellen, who was three years my senior, couldn't understand that we could play as if nothing had happened – but that is what children do.

EVACUATED TO SAFETY

STRANGE as it may seem I was evacuated out of London almost a year before the onset of the Blitz. The government took the threat of war seriously and we lived in fear from the constant warning of air raids from the enemy. Mother would make us sleep under a fortified dining table night after night just in case the Germans dropped bombs on our house. Little did we know at that time that this fear would be realised during the devastating Blitz of London. The first six months of World War Two became nicknamed the 'Phoney War', simply because there was very little fighting and no bombs were actually dropped. Luckily, this gave Britain more time to protect herself and her children from attack. Under the codename 'Operation Pied Piper' my sister Ellen and myself were moved out of London in September 1939, along with another thirty thousand children, to places of safety in the countryside.

ABOVE: Children wait patiently at a train station to be evacuated to the country before the start of World War Two.

I remember the day very clearly as it was 3 September, the day after my eleventh birthday. It was a cloudy, but quite warm day and I sat with my head resting in my hands watching a man painting a pillar box mustard yellow and wondering why. I never had time to ask why, but learned many years later that this was gas-sensitive paint that would change colour in the event of a gas attack. We had sandbags piled up outside our front door and we had already received our issue of gas masks in the event of an attack. Then mother called from the hall to say it was time to go. We had no relatives outside the East End, so Ellen and I had to join the long,

ABOVE: This British family refused to be driven from their home by the Germans' threats. A Union Jack, a pile of sandbags and a handwritten sign saying 'Home Sweet Home' were their messages to the enemy.

snaking line of evacuees waiting to board a train at Waterloo which would take us out of the city and into the unknown.

We had no idea where we were going, all we were told was that we were heading towards the West Country where we would be met by a host family. The West Country, it might as well have been another planet to us kids, we had never set foot outside of the East End. Frightened and yet somehow excited, we stood on the overcrowded platform with brown cardboard labels pinned to our jackets as if we were parcels waiting to be posted. Emotions ran high that day. I think Ellen was more frightened than I was, being older, and it didn't help when I looked up into mother's face and saw tears running down her cheeks. We didn't know how long it would be before we would see her again and the thought suddenly sent terror through me. I grabbed her skirt, my face drained of any colour, and started to sob uncontrollably.

As the train drew into the station all you could hear was the sound of the children being marched towards the empty carriages, singing *The Lambeth Walk* as loud as they could, hoping that it would keep up morale. Most of them were too frightened to talk, including me, and I had to be forcibly removed from my mother's skirt by my guardian who was a teacher from Ellen's school. She tried to be kind, but she must have been frustrated at the number of children she had to try and safely herd onto the train. She held up a banner with the name of the school, and behind her a queue of children followed like frightened sheep. Ellen grabbed hold of

ABOVE: Anyone that could get close to a window or door waved frantically as the train pulled out of Waterloo station.

my hand and gripped it so tightly I remember the feeling of my fingers going numb. We were lucky enough to be near a window so we could look out and wave goodbye to mother who was still crying and yet trying to be brave for our sakes. 'Goodbye darlings, goodbye . . .' but her next words were lost as the steam engulfed her and the train pulled out of the station.

The journey seemed endless and once out of London we passed field after field with nothing except a few cows and sheep. At first it was fascinating, we had only seen pictures of the country so it was all alien to us, but eventually the fascination changed to boredom. We had been allowed to pack two of our favourite toys in our knapsacks, mine were my threadbare teddy called Tommy after my best friend, and a tiny wooden soldier my father had made for me. My sister had also sneaked a pack of Happy Family cards in her case, so we managed to find a space and played until we tired of that, too. I remember pestering Ellen for food, I was always hungry and it seemed hours since we had eaten breakfast. Mother had made sandwiches, given us an apple each and also six barley sugars to suck on the

RIGHT: Great Western Railway poster. Artwork by Frank Newbould.

journey. We made short work of our food and eventually I fell asleep with my head in Ellen's lap.

'Wake up Mary, we're here,' said Ellen shaking my shoulder.

'Where?' I asked.

'I don't rightly know,' she replied. 'Oh hold on, the station sign says Barnstaple, wherever that is!'

Barnstaple turned out to be in North Devon, a beautiful part of the country I have visited many times since as an adult. It didn't seem beautiful on that day – quiet, remote, but not beautiful. Where were the rows and rows of houses and streets with kids playing on every corner? Our carriage was offloaded here and we were all taken by bus to another village called Hartland. I would estimate there were around thirty of us, some dirty and badly dressed, others looking a little smarter as Ellen and myself were. We were all taken to the village hall where we were given a drink of water and told to sit on the floor until our names were called out.

It seemed to take ages before we heard our names and, after getting to our feet, we were walked over to a middle-aged couple who turned out to be a Dr Morris and his wife Dora. They were both quite plump

and I remember thinking how funny the doctor looked with his wispy hair and round spectacles perched on the end of his nose. They were very kind to us as we walked along the narrow country lanes. I remember thinking how dark it was, not a street light in sight. The hedges were so high we couldn't have seen what was on the other side even if we had wanted to. It took us about ten minutes to arrive at the farm, but to tell you the truth I was so sleepy by that time I can't remember a thing about the house so my first impressions will have to be from when I woke in the morning.

I slept soundly after our journey, a sleep that was greatly induced by the comfort of the huge bed Ellen and I shared. I am not sure what woke me up, but I think it was the sound of a rather large rooster announcing it was morning. I blinked my eyes and looked around the room, trying to remember where I was. Everything was strange from the rosebud wallpaper to the pretty wash jug and basin which stood in the corner with a white flannel and a square of soap. I got out of bed and pulled the curtains to be greeted by a beautiful sunny day and nothing in sight except a

ABOVE: Two evacuees arrive at their new home after a long journey from London.

couple of dogs, a herd of cows heading for a large shed and field after field of green.

There was a knock at the door and Ellen told whoever it was to come in. It was the doctor's wife to tell us that breakfast was ready. We quickly washed and dressed and headed downstairs following the amazing cooking smells that wafted up our noses. We were both excited and nervous, but hunger was the thing I remember the most. In the kitchen we were introduced to Mrs Hannington, one of the scariest women I can honestly say I have ever met. She had hair that stood up on end, a rather protruding wart on the side of her nose and very few teeth to her name. She just nodded her head when we were introduced and plonked an amazing plate of food in front of us without saying a word. Sausages, bacon, egg and chunks of freshly cooked bread – I can still taste it today. I think the doctor's wife had seen the expression on our faces when we met Mrs Hannington and told us not to worry about 'cook' and that her bark was much worse than her bite. Of course as a young child I took that quite literally and remember thinking that I

ABOVE: A group of evacuees having an open-air maths lesson in a hayfield near a village in Monmouthshire, Wales.

musn't get on the wrong side of her otherwise she would bite me! She never did, of course, but I don't think I was ever truly comfortable in her company and I used to hide behind a curtain if I met her walking in the hall after dark.

The things I learned during my first week of evacuation were amazing. For example, I never knew milk came from cows and that you had to pull their udders to get it out. This was not something we had been taught at school. Bernard, the farmhand was only too happy to show us round and let us have a go at most things. In fact, after a couple of weeks he said we were starting to be a real couple of country bumpkins and a great help to him. He allowed us to help him collect the cows from the field and guide them down the lane to the barn where they were milked. Bernard and his son held sticks to help guide the cows, so Ellen and I decided to get sticks from the hedgerow to get the cows moving, but we chose some that were so prickly they left our hands looking like pin cushions.

My second shock was that eggs are laid by chickens. That is still one of my greatest memories going round the yard trying to find where the chickens had hidden them and then gently putting them in a straw-lined basket. My final shock was that bacon and sausages were made from pigs, this was a piece of information I am not so sure I wanted to accept but it didn't stop me eating them anyway.

The village school was about half a mile away from the doctor's house and we had to climb two steep hills to get there. We usually arrived late because we were not used to climbing hills and we were prone to dawdling picking wild strawberries

and blackberries to eat on the way. A few times we got a lift from a neighbouring farmer on his tractor, how exciting that was – but of course would not be allowed these days. The kids at the school were friendly on the whole, although there were a couple of girls who used to tease us about our London accents. We enjoyed our days there and I think it must have been quite a shock to mother when we eventually returned home because our skin was tanned and we had bright rosy cheeks from all the exercise, not like the rather greyish appearance that most East End kids had in those days.

The only time I remember actually getting reprimanded by the doctor and his wife was when Ellen and I decided to have a pillow fight after some stupid argument about a boy in the village. I was teasing my sister that she fancied him and she was starting to get angry and hit me with her pillow. I, needless to say, retaliated and hit her back. Unfortunately the pillows were full of feathers and as the seams started to split the room filled up with white down. We had feathers everywhere, in our hair, up our noses, stuck to our lips and the room quickly looked like

it had been hit by a rather heavy snowstorm. Our punishment was to gather all the feathers up and sew them back into the pillows and we weren't allowed the additional treat at teatime of some of cook's gingerbread. I think we felt duly ashamed but I can't remember shedding any tears.

Our time in Devon was a happy experience apart from missing mother and our friends from the East End. The doctor and his wife were quite firm but fair and I will always be grateful to them for showing me a totally different way of life. Unfortunately our time of blissful unawareness was cut short when the doctor's wife went down with pleurisy and had to spend a spell in hospital. The doctor felt it would be better if we were moved to another host family, but mother, like many other parents, decided that the war was never going to happen and London had started to relax. It was a joyful reunion at Waterloo, although the streets of London never seemed quite the same again after those wonderful days on the farm.

When we did eventually get back home our friends did not have such happy stories to tell. Many had been separated from their

siblings and sent to homes that did not treat them like family. They were ostracised by many of the local children and their parents received quite a few harrowing letters asking if they could come home. My friend Tommy was sent to Wales and I remember him saying to me, 'Them Welshes they tried their best to make us feel at 'ome, but to me it could never be 'ome, I felt like I had been dumped in the middle of nowhere and that no one would ever find us again!'

I am still thankful to this day that Ellen and I had the chance to experience country life. It was a shock to the system, but a nice shock and one that taught me there was a world beyond the dingy streets of the East End. And the war – what war? I honestly believe both of us forgot there was going to be a war, except when the

doctor asked if we would like to listen to the radio with him. Those were the times I cried because it made me think of mother and father back home and the thought that our beautiful city might be destroyed.

My sister and I did not get involved in the second evacuation from London, which is a shame because that was when the war really started. Mind you, I wouldn't be able to tell you my experiences both happy and sad had we been whisked away again. I would like to ask mother now why we were not sent away to a safe haven, but she is no longer around to ask. I suspect she heard some of the harrowing stories from some of my friends' parents and decided perhaps it was safer to be at home under her protection.

ABOVE: Happy evacuees rush to greet their parents on their return to London.

FOLLOWING our return to London in April 1940, everyone carried on life as normal and most of us had abandoned our gas masks believing that the war was never going to come. Little did we know how wrong we were. I remember the first day quite vividly. It was a Saturday and Tommy, myself and a crowd of other kids were playing football down our street. We had made goal posts out of neighbour's dustbins and we were equal with two goals each when a man in a suit and titfer [hat] parked right in the middle of our pitch. Cars weren't common on our streets, so rare in fact it made all of us stop playing and stare at the man.

"Ere, mate, you can't park your jam jar [car] there, it's our football pitch,' shouted an outraged Tommy.

'I'm here to visit number 15, young man, do you want to do an old man out of his pension?' the man retorted. He was an insurance salesman who had come to sort out Mr Horton's (from number 15) claim for a disability handout. We

ABOVE: A group of boys playing football in the street.

had to give in and allow the man to park on our 'pitch'. How could we have ever known that in the future you wouldn't be able to move for cars in London. Anyway, back to the point. We were about to break up the game to go our separate ways, when the eerie sound of an air raid siren shattered our childhood chatter.

'Blimey, we'd better scarper, the Germans are coming …' Tommy shouted above the noise. I will never forget those words as long as I live.

I ran as fast as my little legs would carry me back home. I had had the drill drummed into me time and time again, but never did I dream I would ever have to put it into practise or, indeed, so often in the next few weeks. Father had managed to fortify our dining room table as best he could to provide a temporary shelter, although had we had more warning we would have headed to one of the Underground stations where families had been told to collect in the event of an attack.

Some of the kids from the East End of London never experienced evacuation because their parents were not prepared to let them go. In fact many relied on their sons to be the father figure while dad was away fighting for

ABOVE: This is one of the one hundred air raid sirens that were installed in police stations in the City of London and surrounding areas.

Night after night the skies filled with German bombers often escorted by fighter planes during the period of the Blitz – the noise was deafening and their cargo lethal.

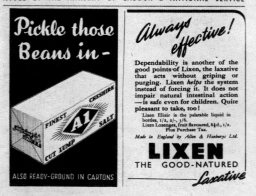

his country. Older girls had to mind their younger siblings while their parents were busy trying to earn their daily crust. These kids had to learn to come to terms with the horror of war and there was no escaping this terror because it was the East End that took the brunt of the bombing. I asked my mother once why we had so many direct hits in our area and she said it was easy for the Luftwaffe, they simply had to follow the route of Thames which led them directly to the docks based at the East End of the city. Despite our best efforts to make everywhere as dark as possible, they still found their targets.

Everywhere there were bomb sites and derelict houses – the streets that were once the kids' playground were now littered with debris, others not recognisable at all. These areas, dangerous though they were, had become the new playgrounds of the East End kids – their hideouts, their gang headquarters and their daily meeting places.

Each day we would choose our meeting places according to the game plan for that day. Sometimes it would be cowboys, sometimes explorers, sometimes soldiers, sometimes firefighters, whatever took our fancy at any particular time. We were never bored, we were just too busy playing despite what was going on around us and it is wonder that any of us survived at all.

One of our favourite playgrounds was an area surrounding Bethnal Green Hospital. There were two places that had been hit and the authorities had fenced them off to keep kids out, we liked to call these the 'small jungle' and the 'big jungle' because both were so overgrown with weeds. It was strange that an area in the East End of London could be so lush and abundant with wildlife. We used to pretend we were on safari and collected beetles, caterpillars and grasshoppers and there was many a time I turned over a rusty old tin can to find a gruesome, hairy looking spider. Inwardly I would scream, but there was no way I was going to let the boys know I was scared. I do remember once, though, during a game of hide and seek concealing myself underneath an old tarpaulin. I quickly gave my hiding place away when some nasty creepy crawlie decided to go up the leg of my shorts.

Thinking back our language was terrible, swearing was just par for the course, probably just picked up from ma and pa when they had a fight. I remember Tommy coming round one morning and asking me what a certain word meant. I had no idea but probably made something up, and out of curiousity asked him why he wanted to know. He said his ma used this word a lot when referring to his dad, so from then on it became our favourite word. We thought nothing of yelling 'Sod off!' or 'Arse'oles!' when some

ABOVE: Firefighters control a blaze after an air raid in Ludgate Hill, in the City of London.

interfering old busybody told us we couldn't play in a certain place. Little did we realise at the time they were only saying it for our own safety.

As kids from working class families we made the most of our environment to create games and toys. Those kids that were lucky enough to have a set of marbles, guarded them as if they were made of a precious metal, well aware that a kid from a rival street would pinch them as soon as their back was turned. Marbles could either be flicked into a hole, or flicked so that they hit another marble. If you managed to hit a marble, it meant that you had won, if not the game continued. Any glass marble that was streaked with red was known as a 'blood alley' and was a much prized possession.

Leap-frog, hopscotch, piggy-back races, jacks, marbles and skipping (mainly for the girls) were the games we played when our parents told us to stay close to home. In winter we used to make slides on the ice and polish it with our backsides to make it as slippery as possible. Old tin trays

ABOVE: Children playing marbles outside a pub.

were our sledges and, if you were lucky enough to live on a hill, you could have wonderful races from the top to the bottom.

Tommy and his brother Johnny made a wonderful go-kart out of a discarded soap box and a pair of old pram wheels. This gave us endless hours of fun and always accompanied us on our adventures. It was rare that kids from another street joined in our games, as children tended to band together in gangs according to where they lived. We often had younger siblings tag along with us though, because it was the responsibility of our older friends to mind their brothers and sisters when they were not in school. I was the youngest and was quite capable of taking care of myself, so I was not hindered by child minding. My sister, far too grown-up to join in our street games, spent most of her time reading or making clothes for herself as she was starting to go through that 'boy stage', something I could not understand at the time. Boys were fun, but kissing them – yuck – you must be joking!

I was definitely a tomboy and felt more comfortable in the company of the boys. However, sometimes at school Tommy would go off and play separately and then I would join in the more mundane skipping games. We would have a long rope with a girl at each end and play the 'in and out' game, where children ran into a turned rope, jumped once or twice and then had to run out again without touching the rope. We also played a game called 'pepper', which was when the rope was turned very fast so that one jump traversed two spins of the rope. While we were skipping we used to chant 'Salt, vinegar, mustard, pepper'

and as we said the last word, the girls turned the rope faster and faster.

One rope game that the boys would join in, was called 'Higher and Higher'. This is where the rope is held still and the children jump over it one at a time. The rope would be raised a little after each round until one person remained having jumped the highest without touching the rope. Other rhymes we chanted when skipping included:

Do you know last night and the night before
Three tom cats came knocking at my door
One had a fiddle, one had a drum
And one had a pancake sticking to its bum!

That last line always made us giggle, no matter how many times we sang it. Another favourite with us East End kids was the game of 'Spuds'. Players would stand in a line or a circle with their fists clenched tightly and held out in front of them at waist height. One person would count off, hitting each fist with their own and chanting: 'One potato, two potato, three potato, four; five potato, six potato, seven potato, more. O-U-T spells out'. When the letter 'T' was called, that person had to put one hand behind their back. The game carried on until only one 'spud' remained and they were claimed the winner.

Ball games were very popular and were always played up against a wall. Many a time someone who was trying to sleep after a late night shift would yell at us or throw a bucket of water out of the window. It was great fun trying to dodge the water, but usually we moved along to another

ABOVE: Three children sharing a skipping rope in a street as there was often only one rope to go round all of us.

wall out of respect. We weren't all bad! There were various moves in ball games – 'unders and overs' which was throwing the ball overarm or underarm, or 'dropsies' which meant you let the ball hit the ground and clapped your hands before catching it again. Each ball game was accompanied by a rhyme, just like skipping and the one I remember vividly was:

> *One, two, three, O'Lara*
> *I saw my auntie Clara*
> *Sitting on her bumtiara*
> *Eating chocolate biscuits.*

One game my friend and I played involved bouncing the ball hard and having to lift your leg over it before catching it again. This meant we had to tuck our dresses into our knicker elastic so that the ball wasn't restricted and this always made the boys snigger. We had to do the same when we were doing handstands or cartwheels and I usually got a clip round the ear if my mother caught me with my skirt tucked up as she said, 'It wasn't right that a young lady should show her knickers in public!'

As you can see without televison, computers, video games and very little room to play indoors, we had to look far and wide for our fun and make use of every available plot of land that the Germans hadn't totally destroyed. We would spend some time every day picking up bits of shrapnel which we could sell to the local scrap

merchants for a few pennies. We certainly made the most of what we had and, looking back, there are more happy memories than sad. The truly sad times were when we learned that a family had been killed during a bombing raid, amazingly none from our own street, but I did lose one very close friend, Amelia, who lived just two streets away when their house was destroyed by fire.

Tommy's dad was also a firefighter and I remember the pride on Tommy's face when he was asked to go and help one night during a raid when there were just not enough hands to go round. Several kids helped that night, risking their lives by holding the enormous hoses as close as possible to the flames. I remember seeing them walking home the next morning exhausted, their faces black and streaked where the water had sprayed them. I think that night Tommy turned from a boy into a man. I didn't get to speak to him until later the next day but he told me it was terrifying and he didn't know how our fathers coped with the job night after night. Brave men indeed, risking their lives to try and salvage as much as they could of our precious East End of London.

I do know that the East End, although rough in appearance, was a place of trust. Few people ever locked their front door and if they did the key was always hanging on a piece of string just within reach from the letterbox. The communities looked out for one another and as kids we were always welcome in one another's houses. I remember walking into Tommy's house one afternoon – we never bothered to knock – and hearing voices from the parlour walked in to find his grandad sitting in a tin bath in front of the fire taking his weekly ablutions. I don't know who was most red in the face – him or me!

Well that was my East End of London, a special place, somewhere we all loved and never wanted to leave. We had all heard of Hitler and I had seen him on the newsreels at the cinema, but I couldn't quite understand then why one man should want to destroy the city in which I lived. I would like to bring back that community spirit today, but I would hate it to be war that made it that way again.

ABOVE: Photograph by John Hinde of an ARP warden. Hinde was an important early exponent of colour photography in Britain.

TAKING

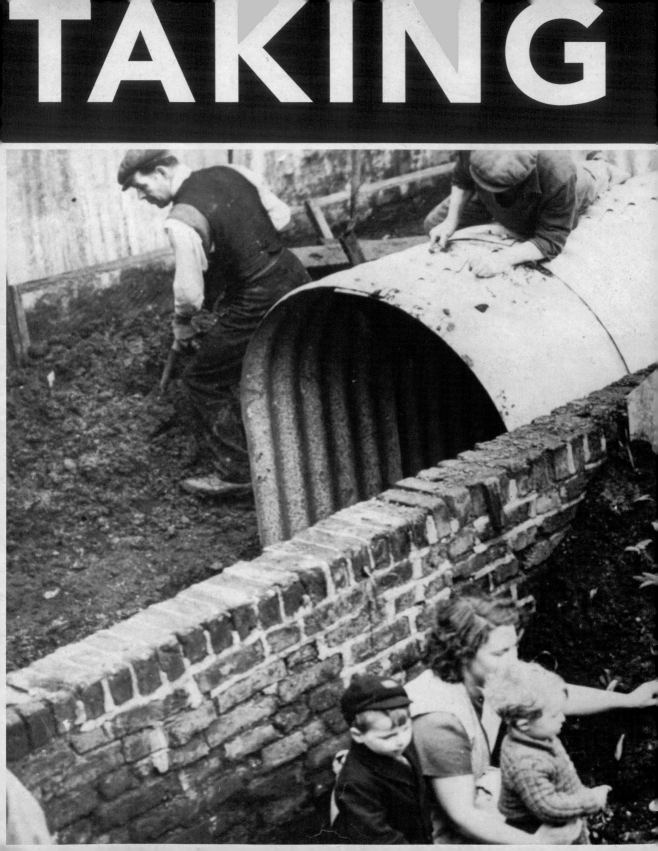

SHELTER

FOR two shillings a yard, you could buy thick blackout material, and this is what mother had to do to make sure that not a gleam of light escaped our windows and doors. I remember at the start of the Blitz mother was even afraid to strike a match, just in case it led the Germans to our door. The streets were pitch black, as the street lights were either switched off completely, dimmed or shielded so that their light reflected down. Our street was one of those where the street lights were turned off completely and many people were injured from tripping up, falling down steps or bumping into things they

just couldn't see. Even cars – few though they were – had to have hoods over their headlights and people were advised to wear something white so that drivers could see them. There were many accidents during the blackout, especially cars colliding simply because they simply couldn't see each other, it really wasn't a safe time to go out. Mother used to say it was only criminals and lovers who enjoyed the blackout.

Firewatchers and street wardens had to stay awake all night listening for the sounds of planes threatening London. One man, a Mr Hanley, who lived right on the end of our street was often

ABOVE: The government made sure there was enough blackout material for every household and cheap enough for even the poorest families. In most cases it was a black cotton fabric that could be bought on the roll.

put on listening duty. I never understood why, he was practically stone deaf and you had to shout at him just to be heard.

As soon as the sirens sounded, mothers would grab their children and run out to the Anderson shelter in their garden. We were lucky enough to get one of these three weeks into the Blitz, which we shared with our neighbours, the Baileys, and their two children. To try and brighten up an otherwise rather dull structure, Mr Bailey had put flowery wallpaper inside, a couple of pictures of the seaside and was attempting to grow some flowers on the roof. Each time we went in the shelter mother always grabbed a large brown paper bag which, I assumed, contained some food to see us through the night. It was only when I peeked inside one night hoping to sneak a sandwich, that I discovered it contained our birth certificates, father's Post Office saving book, a first-aid kit and some other personal items which she didn't want to be destroyed in the event of our house being hit.

One night I remember vividly because I woke to find myself alone in the Anderson shelter. I had wrapped myself up in a blanket as usual and curled up on the floor because I was always tired after a day at school. I woke to find the door to the shelter banging and the sound of some people shouting outside. Apparently a house directly behind us in an adjoining street had taken a direct hit, and everyone had gone out to see how much damage there was. That was apart from

me, who had apparently slept through the whole thing.

As I emerged into the dark I remember seeing people frantically digging at the rubble with their bare hands and seeing two men carrying a stretcher covered with a red blanket. Amazingly no one was killed in that house that night, which showed the Morrison table installed in their front room had taken the brunt of the damage. One of the children had a crushed leg and the mother had to be taken away suffering from concussion, but they had survived.

The Morrison shelter was an indoor table shelter assembled from a kit and then bolted together inside the house. The steel top doubled as a table and each side had wire mesh panels, one of which contained a door. This type of shelter was issued to people who did not have a garden and got its name from the Minister for Home Security, Mr Herbert Morrison. They

ABOVE: Clementine Churchill, the wife of the wartime prime minister, Winston Churchill, is pictured with the home secretary, Herbert Morrison while they conduct an official visit together .

were approximately 2 metres (6 ft 6 in) long and 1.2 metres (4 ft) wide and 0.75 metres (2 ft 6 in) high, so they weren't ideal places to hide if you were claustrophobic.

The Anderson shelter, although larger (designed to hold up to six people), was dark and damp and many people became reluctant to use them. They were made out of corrugated iron sheets which were bolted together at the top with steel plates at either end. They were half buried in a hole in the ground and then partially covered with earth. This type of shelter was free to anyone who earned less than £5 a week and by September 1939, there were over one and a half million Anderson shelters erected in gardens around the country. The Anderson shelter could withstand anything but a direct hit, but it was hard to sleep because they did not muffle the sound of the bombs. There was a bucket in the corner of our shelter just in case someone couldn't make it through the night, but we all held on as long as possible as no one wanted to make a fool of themselves. There is no doubt that despite their discomfort, risk of flooding and lack of room, both the Anderson and Morrison shelters did save many lives.

ABOVE: Many people took their most treasured belongings inside their Anderson shelters in case their house was totally destroyed.

By the autumn of 1940, the government started to realise that these shelters on the surface did not afford much protection from high explosive bombs and they announced that many London underground stations were to be opened up as air raid shelters. Mind you this decision was forced by the fact that thousands of East Enders had already taken it into their own hands to use these stations as shelter anyway. These became popular refuges during the long nights of bombing and people came armed with blankets, sandwiches, thermos flasks and pillows, and you could usually see a child clutching a beloved teddy bear that they weren't prepared to leave behind to face the perils. I always made sure I had my rag doll, which my grandmother had so lovingly made when I was born. Mind you, being a tomboy, I kept it well hidden beneath my jumper if Tommy happened to be around. People tended to feel safe in the undergrounds and found comfort in the large number of friends around them; often as many as sixty thousand people would descend on the Underground stations – and here a community was born.

I have one vivid memory of taking shelter during the Blitz and that was after a bomb had blasted Bank station making East Enders realise that perhaps the tube was not the safest place to be during a raid. A crowd took the matter into their own hands and formed an astonishing shelter which became known as Mickey's Shelter. We ran with the crowds through the streets, petrified

ABOVE: Because of the nightly bombing raids, many people from the more densely populated parts of London sleep in underground stations for safety .

as the sirens wailed all around us. The crowd merged at Brushfield Street, Spitalfields, at the old Fruit and Wool Exchange. Beneath the Exchange were massive vaults which it was estimated could hold as many as five thousand people. However, on this particular night I have heard there were twice that number who crammed themselves into that black hole and by 7.30 that evening every inch of floor space had been taken up. The air in the vault quickly became rank and the smell of urine made me heave. Mother tied a handkerchief around my face to try and cut out the smell, but it was difficult to remain calm as it was so dark that we couldn't see anything except vague shapes. There was absolutely no room to move, so once you found your spot you had to stay there whether you liked it or not. Uncomfortable? yes, unhygienic? yes, but safe. Eventually we learned to shut out what was around us. I can't say it was a pleasant experience, but it was the actions of these East Enders that forced the government to build some specially designed deep shelters. However, their offer was a little too late, by the time the first one was finished the Blitz was well and truly over. I never even asked how Mickey's Shelter got its name, but curiosity got the better of me when I started my recollections of the war. Apparently, it was named after an optician called Mickey, who had the intuition to start his own shelter committee and, thanks to him, conditions were improved greatly and many lives were saved.

Another place that people used for shelter were the Tilbury Arches in Stepney. Below the arches were a series of underground cellars used for storing goods which were commandeered by the local council and made into a large public shelter for three thousand people. Needless to say the number who actually sheltered there far exceeded this number and, like Mickey's Shelter, there was no sanitation and Tommy described it as the 'Tilbury hell hole'.

My last memory of sheltering during one of the frequent air raids was the night my sister asked if I would like to go to the cinema to see *Gone With the Wind*. This was a rare treat for me because usually Ellen would not be seen dead in my company, but she had been given some money for her birthday and she must have taken pity on me as one of my close friends had just had to have his leg amputated.

This upset me greatly and gave me nightmares for several weeks afterwards. On this particular night, we went to the Ritz in Lower Clapton and the film had only been running for about twenty minutes when the air raid sirens went off. I started to cry and said it wasn't fair, so Ellen put her arm around my shoulder and made the brave (if not stupid) decision to stay and see the entire film. We ignored the alerts which flashed up on the screen several times and remained in our seats. I would have estimated that half the occupants of the cinema left, but we sat holding hands throughout the film even though we could could feel the vibrations as bombs landed on nearby buildings. Luckily the Ritz remained standing and we were unhurt, but we had a severe ticking off from mother when we returned home. She had been so worried she wouldn't leave the house and sat in the cupboard under the stairs just praying that she would hear the front door open. I remember to this day, the look of relief on her face as she pulled us both close to her chest.

It would be fair to say that the residents of the East End of London suffered more than the more affluent areas of the city. The buildings of the West End were more strongly built than our Victorian terraces, so when the bombs did start to fall there was far less damage. Many of London's more well-to-do families simply shut up their town houses and moved to their second homes in the country until the worst of the war was over. The East Enders, most of whom were doing important work for the war effort, were forced to remain and perhaps that is why our memories of the Blitz are still so vivid.

ABOVE: A committee meeting in 'Mickey's Shelter', an improvised air raid shelter in the vaults under the Fruit and Wool Exchange in Brushfield Street, Spitalfields.

MY FATHER THE
FIREFIGHTER

AS I mentioned earlier, London was bombed for fifty-seven consecutive days and nights by the Nazi Luftwaffe and night after night enormous land mines, incendiaries and even parachute mines endeavoured to destroy the city in which I lived. These explosive devices left behind them a trail of fires and most nights the Fire Services were stretched to breaking point. Although pushed to the point of sheer exhaustion, somehow these brave men and women managed to keep going and quenched as many fires as was humanly possible. They were aware that the raging fires provided the Germans with a marker for yet more raids, so they fought with every last bit of strength they had inside them to put them out. Many times the fires were raging out of control and their lives were not only threatened by the fire itself but from the buildings as they collapsed around them. In the first three weeks of the Blitz, the London firefighters fought over ten thousand fires.

ABOVE: Firemen who met the lord privy seal C. R. Attlee on his visit to the London Fire Service.

Among these brave souls was my father, Eddie, who was a member of the Auxiliary Fire Service (AFS). The AFS had over 200,000 members by the end of 1939, but it was not the sophisticated fire service of today with their up-to-the-minute equipment and speedy fire engines. Many only had pumps that had to be towed to the site by cars or, as in the case of my uncle, an old black taxi cab painted grey to get him to the spot because equipment was in such short supply. It wasn't unusual for my father to work for forty hours without taking a break and at night they were joined by part-time volunteers, many of whom had little or no experience of fighting fires. Women played their role as well and my auntie served as a volunteer with the fire service, not actually fighting fires, but staffing communication centres, riding bikes between the men to pass messages and helping serve on some of the mobile canteens to keep the firefighters going.

My father vividly recalled being called to the docks one Tuesday night to put out a massive fire. He said that bombs were falling all around them when the firefighters arrived, but he tried his hardest to put it to the back of his mind and to concentrate on the job. 'As soon as one fire subsides, another rose out of the wreckage, but we knew we had to try and save the docks.'

Surrounding the docks were the narrow streets where the workers lived. They were rows of small, two-storey houses that could have been knocked over by a strong gust of wind let alone the full power of a Nazi bomb. By half-past six that evening entire streets were a mass of dust and rubble. The fires that resulted from the bombing followed quickly and

provided an unmissable beacon for the next wave of bombers. Even from a distance a great red column of smoke towered into the sky, a terrifying site for Londoners but a welcome sight for the Luftwaffe. My father, exhausted from hours of fighting the fires, sat down with his head in his hands and thought … 'it appeared that the whole of London was burning!'

A shout from a fellow worker brought him back to his senses and he found a new wave of strength to fight the next blaze. The blaze in the warehouse was the largest he had ever encountered and the heat from it was so intense that it blistered the paint on the fireboats trying to pass on the opposite bank of the river. My father had been told to keep his hose on the stocks of timber to try and prevent them from catching fire. It was all too hopeless though, they merely hissed steam, immediately became dry and burst into flame anyway. The warehouses at the docks were a nightmare in themselves because you were never sure what they

ABOVE: Firefighters direct their hoses onto a blazing building after an incendiary raid on the City of London during the Blitz.
RIGHT: An ARP (Air Raid Precautions) poster encouraging people to join the Auxiliary Fire Service.

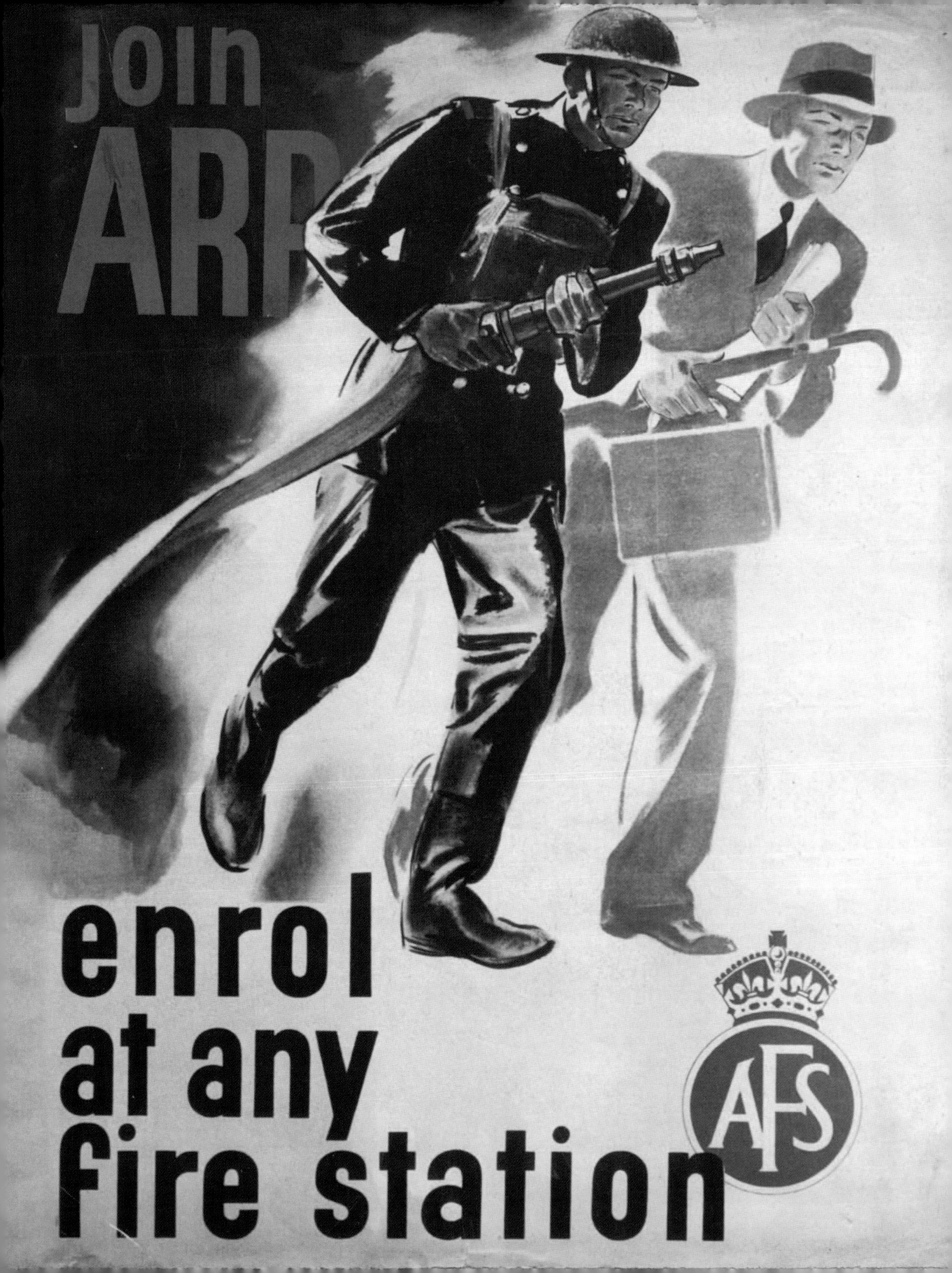

join
ARP

enrol
at any
fire station

AFS

contained. Sometimes their contents were so volatile that they exploded much like the bombs themselves. At the far end was one containing large quantities of rubber tyres. The black clouds of smoke were so asphyxiating that they could only be fought from a distance and even then the firefighters were still constantly choking. Added to all this, were the rats – hordes of them that were fleeing in all directions to avoid being burned to death.

So how did these firefighters cope? 'It wasn't easy,' my father told me many years after the war was over. 'The main thing was keeping a brave face, none of us wanted to show our colleagues that we were bricking it! You looked around you and saw your mates fighting their hardest and you just knew that you couldn't let any of them down. I used to try and crack a few corny jokes just to keep up my own morale and that of my colleagues. I remember one fire at Rum Wharf in the East India dock area, was so large we had no need to use our headlights as we approached. We made a feeble attempt to put it out, but what chance did we have against such a raging inferno. We stood for hours directing our hoses at the flames, sometimes in the same position for hours on end, when we eventually stood up or moved I remember physically crying out with the pain. In spite of the pain and the numbness in our arms and legs from the coldness of the water, we tirelessly fought the fires trying to ignore what was going on around us. People were being constantly evacuated to safety and women carrying children and large bundles streamed away from the danger zone. Strangely I remember a flock of pigeons

ABOVE: Firemen on the roof of Cannon Street Station looking towards St Paul's Cathedral, London.

circling over our heads for about half an hour, seemingly dazed by the smoke and bright sky, perhaps a little confused about what time of day it was. When dawn did come, usually around six o'clock, the Germans ceased their blitz and we were given the "all clear" to go home as the relief crews had come to take over. Somehow we found that last bit of strength to hoist the rolled-up length of hose onto our shoulders and return home to our loved ones.

Perhaps we were the lucky ones, the kids from the homes of the East London dockers could only return to bricks and rubble. Their once shabby furniture had been reduced to ashes and in most cases it was the only home they had ever known. The local vicar had been out all night during the raids, trying to help his flock. He ran from street to street, his lips trembling, his eyes filled with tears as he discovered many of his close friends had been killed or badly injured. That morning I accompanied the vicar to a local school where many of the dockers' families were sheltering. The over-crowded school contained many families that had been bombed out on previous nights, and they waited pitifully for some sort of transport to take them away from their misery. The exhausted mothers pleaded for information and reassurance, but unfortunately there was no answer other than "Would you like another cup of tea?"

One other job I had to deal with as a firefighter was rescuing a German pilot from his aircraft after it had been shot down. I remember desperately trying to pull the man out from the burning wreckage that contained live ammunition and an unexploded bomb. I knew that we could be blown to smitherines any minute. I remember once being asked why I bothered to risk my life to save someone who was intent on finishing mine. To tell you the truth at the time I didn't see it that way, it was just someone that was in trouble that needed a helping hand. I would like to think that the man would have done the same for me if the roles were reversed.

I don't think my wife ever got over the site of my blackened skin and soaked clothing, but she never said anything other than give me a kiss on the cheek and to help me get ready for a bath and bed. Being a firefighter was a hard job and the Blitz made it even harder. Our equipment, and uniforms, were both inadequate and we had to make do with what we had. Our helmets were metal that had been painted black and down the back hung what can only be described as a 'curtain' to protect the back of our necks and our hair from the flames. Neither our jackets or trousers were fire- or heatproof and, being made of thick wool, were extremely heavy. Of course being wool they were extremely absorbent and soaked up every drop of water which made them even heavier. Our boots were made of black leather which became extremely slippery when wet; we found it really difficult to stay on our feet at times. We were constantly coughing from smoke inhalation as we weren't equipped with any special breathing apparatus, the only protection we did have were our gas masks.

Although they were tough times I can still recall how "alive" I felt and my job somehow seemed to be totally rewarding. We were frequently called to normal house fires, too, because people used candles or lamps during the blackout and of course everyone had open fires in those days. One of the most common house fires were in the chimneys where there was a build up of soot; we quickly put these out because we didn't want to make it even easier for the Germans to find us.'

By the time the war ended, over one thousand firefighters had lost their lives and of course thousands of others were injured. My father and all of his colleagues can indeed feel proud to have been such a major part of the war effort and risking their lives every day to save the lives of others.

ABOVE: New Bridge Street in the City of London after a night raid by German bombers.

MY cousin, Sylvia, was training to be a nurse at Lambeth Hospital when the Blitz started and, like for the rest of us, the wail of the sirens and the drone of German bombers became a regular part of her daily life. She was used to seeing sights that would turn the stomachs of most people, but the injuries sustained during the Blitz were perhaps the most horrifying. She told me about one particular night that is etched on her memory to this day and as I listened I can imagine just how frightened the patients and staff must have been.

In her own words, Sylvia recalls the horror of that one particular night. 'I was on duty in the casualty department dressing a wound that one of the doctors had just treated, when I heard a strange whooshing sound. Suddenly the hospital window imploded and my nurse's cap was blown off my head landing on a bed on the far side of the room. Around twenty nurses were killed that night including a new friend I had made called Irene who had only been in England for three months after being transferred from Dublin. The lights had gone out and I had to use a torch which I always had hanging from my belt just for such an emergency. The bomb had caused a lot of damage, destroying two entire wards, the kitchen, dining rooms and laundry as well as damaging three other ward blocks. Lambeth was one of the largest municipal hospitals in London during the war and could accommodate 1,250 patients. Because they had to treat so

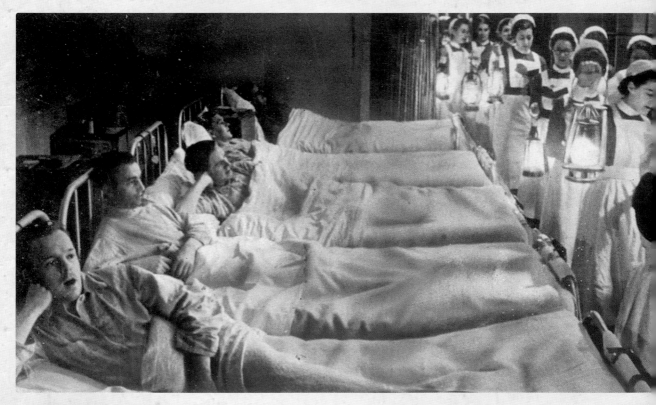

many air raid casualties during the Blitz, many of the elderly and long-term patients had to be moved to smaller hospitals.

Due to the extent of the damage, a decision had to be made quickly. Any of the patients that were strong enough to be moved were evacuated to safer areas and I followed the instructions of one of my superiors who had taken over as temporary commander. One by one the patients were moved to the old workhouse infirmary in the grounds of the hospital. Amazingly no one panicked, no one asked to be moved first and not one patient attempted to get out of bed. I think it was their calmness that kept me focused even though we were trying to douse flames using anything that would hold water. I am not a particularly religious person, but I do remember saying a little prayer that night and somehow the message must have got through because we only lost five patients. The only time I lost my composure was when one of the senior nurses, a woman called Susan Bletchley, ran back into the hospital to try and salvage some of the linen. She

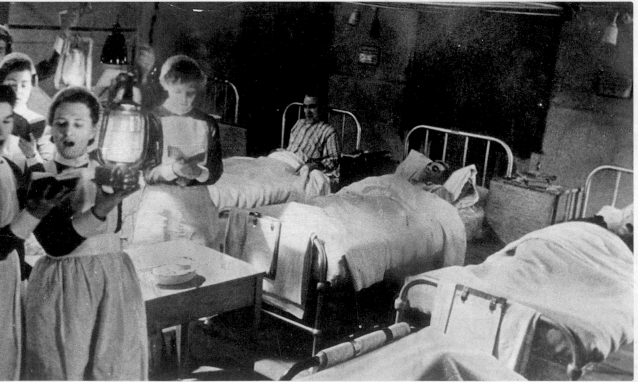

ABOVE: To keep up morale nurses used to sing Christmas carols to the wounded soldiers. Those that were well enough would join in, those that were too weak could be seen to tap a finger, so the music had an effect on everyone.

MAKE NURSING YOUR WAR JOB

—it's War Work with a future

FOR FURTHER PARTICULARS APPLY TO
THE NURSING SECTION · COUNTY HALL · WESTMINSTER BRIDGE · S·E

was overcome by smoke and never made it out of the building; this really upset me and I had to be comforted by another nurse before I could carry on with my duties.

Although the conditions in the original hospital were by no means state of the art, I remember being quite shocked to find out that we now had to work on bare boards, using old, uncomfortable iron bedsteads and a very primitive sluice that could only cope with about forty patients.

We managed to divide the infirmary into two wards which had a mixture of men and women many of whom had suffered injuries during a raid. Also in the wards were patients suffering from tuberculosis, syphilis, cancer, chronic respiratory problems, other chronic diseases and of course lots of children. These were the hardest to deal with in terms of emotion, I never got used to seeing a little boy or girl lying shellshocked against the white sheets after having had a limb amputated. We also had to deal with premature babies which were common during the war because the mother was suffering from shock. We had no special incubators or premature baby units, we had to make do and improvise. I remember helping matron once with a tiny baby weighing just 3 lb 2 oz (1.5 kg) who was having difficulty in breathing on its own. She asked me

LEFT: MAKE NURSING YOUR WAR JOB – a government poster to encourage young women to train as nurses.

to wrap the baby in some damp cotton wool and then to lay it in an old baking tin that had been sterilised. This tin was then placed inside another which contained warm water which was then placed inside an open oven on the lowest setting possible to try and create some steam. Within ten minutes the baby was coping and managed to breathe on its own. Today that sounds so archaic, but we had to use any method possible to try and save a life and amazingly that little baby survived.

One of my jobs as a junior was to delouse patients, many of whom had become infected while sheltering in underground stations. I caught lice twice myself, something which I found quite hard to come to terms with as it made me feel really dirty. I also had to help with washing soiled laundry because the hospital laundry had been bombed. We had no gloves to protect our hands and I remember how sore and cracked they became even though I constantly rubbed them with petroleum jelly. I was always conscious of them whenever I had to change a dressing or give a bed bath, I was convinced the patient would think I had some sort of dreadful skin disease.

The kitchen in the infirmary still had the original old black gas stove and it was here that the junior nurses had to cope with feeding the sick. As a trainee I was often sent there to prepare breakfast so that the day nurses could serve it as soon as they arrived. We had to cut slice after slice of bread and cover it with a meagre layer of margarine. We also had to mix the dried egg powder and make the porridge which, although it sounds very unappetising, was always welcome although I often had a job encouraging the children to eat.

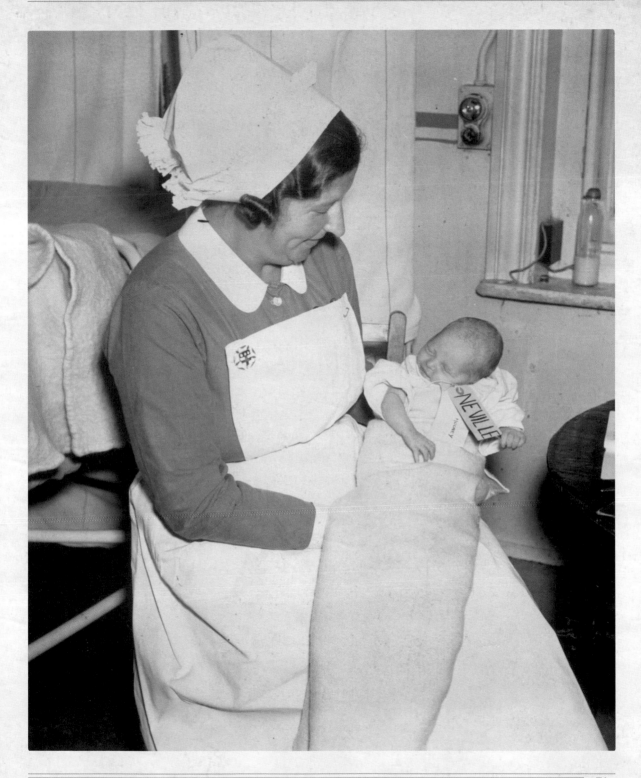

ABOVE: Little Neville Mooney of Fulham, the first baby born in London after the declaration of war, in the arms of a nurse at Queen Charlotte Maternity Hospital.

ABOVE: Two members of the Women's Auxiliary Ambulance Service in Fulham, London.

Nurses that were doing a night shift were given a free meal which arrived in a type of billycan. When I say billycan, it was in fact just four separate tins held together with a spike through the centre. Each layer contained a different course, for example sardines and potatoes, a paltry salad of just lettuce and beetroot and a pudding of custard with something unidentifiable floating in it. It wasn't very appetising but we were always starving and it was free, so we usually ate everything as we couldn't guarantee when we would get our next food or drink.

During blackout ambulances and other forms of makeshift transport arrived with more patients. Many were dead on arrival and it was down to the matron to inform the relatives. Matron would do her nightly rounds carrying her hurricane lamp; I know I was always in awe of this woman who seemed to have nerves of steel. If there was a lull in the bombing, we got patients who were well enough to make dressings. These were then packed into large steel drums and sterilised by using autoclaving. This method involved subjecting the contents to high pressure steam for about thirty minutes. Cleanliness

was our main priority because we couldn't risk septicaemia and cross infections in the primitive conditions in which we were expected to work.

One thing the war did was to accelerate the use of penicillin. The very nature of the war produced such appalling casualties that the medical profession were faced with an enormous challenge to prevent the spread of disease. Researchers speeded up their tests and even though pencillin had been discovered before the war, it took the conflict to make companies develop ways of producing it on a large scale. One of the first times that pencillin was used en masse was after D-Day when so many men were at risk from gangrene due to the length of time they would have to wait to see a surgeon. Prior to the use of penicillin, a wound could fester in just a few hours.

On one occasion I was asked to accompany a patient who was being taken by ambulance to Dartford Hospital. The man had sustained major injuries when he had dived in front of a car to save a toddler and had fractures to his jaw, arms, legs and pelvis and was in a lot of pain. We did not have the facilities to treat him at Lambeth and so he

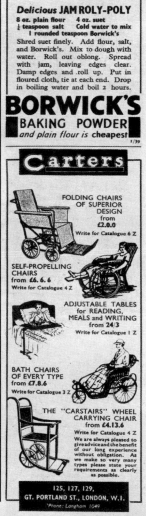

had to be moved. I was just one of the nurses that accompanied him that day and we took turns holding his hand and talking to him to take his mind of his discomfort. My mother joined the ARP as an ambulance driver and I remember she was always exhausted after her shifts which lasted eight hours at a time. It made it especially hard because they had to drive during the blackout which put extra strain on the eyes as they had to peer into the darkness to make sure they weren't bumping into anything, including humans. The job she hated the most was cleaning the interior of the ambulance after carrying casualties, she told me this upset her stomach far more than actually dealing with any of the wounded. It was also her responsibility to check the tyres, radiator and battery every morning to make sure the ambulance would always be ready for the next emergency.

I lived about one mile from the hospital and after my shift I would don my metal helmet, carry my gas mask over my arm and drag my weary legs back to the nurses' home. One particular morning I was walking along eating an apple I had saved from my night's rations when I noticed that a whole row of terraced houses opposite the hospital were no longer there. I had been so wrapped up with the damage at the hospital I never once considered what had happened in the immediate vicinity. I realised these were people's homes when I went on duty, on my return they had nothing.'

ABOVE: A London hospital for the aged and infirm was hit during a bombing raid.

Little people like big plates of BIRD'S CUSTARD ... they like its special flavour and adore its golden creaminess. And from early days it is good for them ... for BIRD'S is light, satisfying, easily digested. Serve BIRD'S every day at one meal or another.

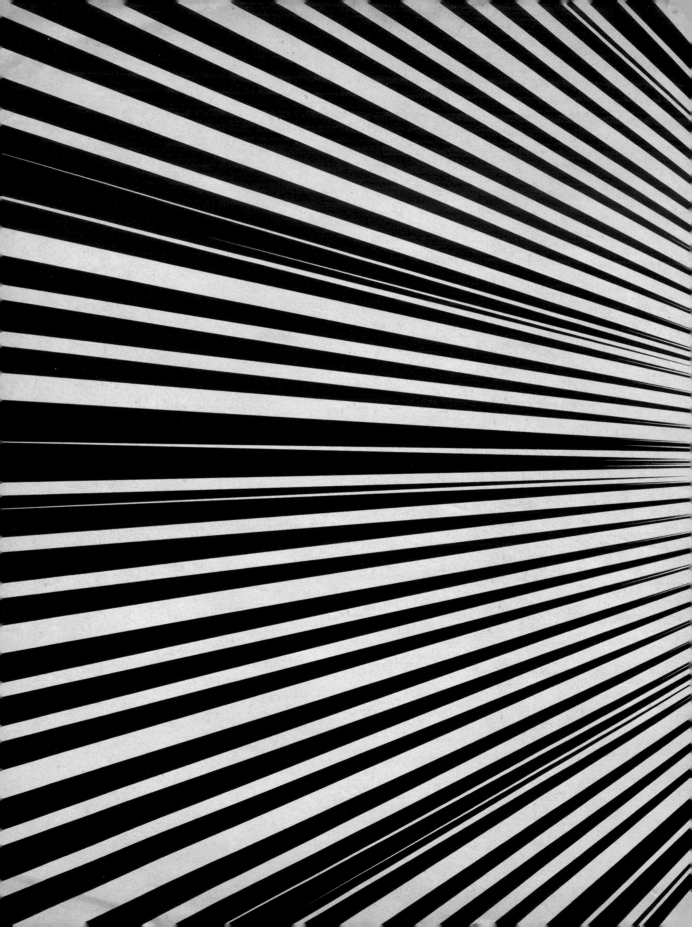

THE

BETHNAL GREEN

TUBE DISASTER

AT the age of sixteen, Tommy's brother Peter, was just old enough to be an Air Raid Precautions (ARP) messenger and on the night of Wednesday, 3 March 1943, he was running errands for the emergency services. Even though the Blitz had ended almost two years previously, the East End was still a target for Hitler's revenge. Tommy had been sitting listening to the radio with his mother when it suddenly went dead, this was often a sign that there was about to be a raid. This was confirmed when Peter came running into the house and told his family to take shelter. Their choice on that evening was the Underground Station at Bethnal Green, being one of the few deep-level stations in the East End of London. It was situated in a densely populated part of the East End and often housed as many as seven thousand people during a raid. It was a popular place to go as it contained five thousand bunk beds which meant you stood a chance of getting a good night's sleep.

On this particular evening there were many people in the vicinity of Bethnal Green aware that there might be a retaliatory raid following heavy bombing of Hitler's Berlin on 1 March. By the time Tommy and his mother reached the station there were already around five hundred people who had taken shelter down below. The sirens started to forecast a raid at around 8.15 p.m. and, aware that the Germans had switched tactics and started using faster bombers, the residents of Bethnal Green and surrounding areas knew they had less time to reach the shelter.

The station only had one dimly-lit entrance from the street, from which a flight of nineteen

ABOVE: One of the familiar communal air raid shelter signs found around London during World War II.

stone steps led down to the first landing. It had been raining so the steps were slippery, difficult for an able-bodied person to negotiate in good light, let alone young and old having to find their way by the light of a single 25-watt bulb. There was no central handrail to guide people to the next set of seven steps which would take them into the ticket hall. From there, a set of escalators took them the eighty foot to the safety of the platforms below.

It is estimated there were as many as fifteen hundred people negotiating the first set of steps at around 8.20 p.m. and Tommy and his mother were right in the midst of them trying desperately to stay on their feet. They knew the place like the back of their hands as they had used the station as a bedroom for a couple of years now. They were used to queuing, that was all a normal part of war, but they weren't prepared for the mayhem that was about to take place.

On the other side of the street from the station entrance, a searchlight was making its arc in the sky. About half a mile away in Victoria Park, an anti-aircraft unit was getting ready to practice firing a brand new rocket weapon for the first time. At exactly 8.27 p.m.

Victoria Park sent its new rockets into the air letting out a frightening roar. This was an unfamiliar sound to the people trying to get into Bethnal Green station and very quickly apprehension turned to complete panic as someone yelled 'It's a bomb!'. Everyone started pushing the people in front of them and a woman carrying a small child slipped on the damp steps causing a major domino effect as people started to fall on top of one another. Within a period of just a few seconds it is estimated that hundreds of people fell. The people queuing outside were completely unaware of what had happened inside and consequently kept surging forwards, desperate to reach the shelter of the underground. There were screams, moans, whimpers and then it all went quiet. The floor was very quickly a pile of bodies all the way back to street level. Adults fell on children, children fell on the elderly until people just simply ran out of breath. Anyone clutching a child to their body for safety, quite literally squeezed the life out of them as more and more bodies piled on top of them. Tommy was the first to hear the screams and grabbed his mother's hand. They

had already made their way to the ticket hall before the first lady fell, but they both froze to the spot as they realised what was happening right in front of their eyes.

Down in the depths of the station around one thousand people were already bedding down for the night, totally unaware of the chaos above them. The queue continued to push forward, too frightened to stay outside for fear of being blown apart. Instead of starting the descent down the stairs they found they were standing on a human platform of bodies. Because of the panic, any rescue attempts were severely hampered and Tommy distinctly remembered a policeman crawling over the top of the amassed bodies to see the extent of the disaster. He climbed out about five minutes later, ashen faced with tears running down his cheeks. He sent for help before returning to the depths to help extricate people from the tangle of arms and legs below.

ABOVE: An underground tube shelter which was built in the Shepherd's Bush Studios, London.

Despite the best efforts of the brave rescuers, 173 people died in the panic – 27 men, 84 women and 62 children. A further 62 people had to be taken to hospital and, added to that, it was all totally unnecessary. There never were any enemy planes overhead, it was simply a military practice that had scared the living daylights out of the people in Bethnal Green that night.

Tommy who was pinned up against the wall by the number of people in the ticket hall, remembered being grabbed by a rather large ARP lady who pushed her way through the crowd, took hold of his arms and told him to go down below and not say a word about what had happened. Tommy had lost sight of his mother and fearful that she had got caught up in the melée sat shaking against the cold wall of Bethnal Green station platform. He was eventually reunited with his mother a few hours later but many others were not so lucky.

The government, scared that such a disaster would destroy public morale, they decided that the whole affair at Bethnal Green should be hushed up. After a secret enquiry the War Cabinet decided that any subsequent publication of the disaster 'would give the incident a disproportionate importance and might encourage the enemy to make further nuisance raids'. Instead of a public enquiry, the government issued a report saying that action was being taken to prevent further such disasters taking place.

When the crowds emerged the following morning there was no evidence whatsoever that a disaster had taken place. There were no reports in the newspapers, and the steps had been washed to remove any evidence. The official account was simply that a woman had tripped carrying a baby and that a few people had fallen on top of her. The East End was a close-knit community and everyone knew someone who was involved or had been affected by the disaster. The steps are still there to this day, although they have been painted and a safety rail has been added. On the corner of Cambridge Heath Road and Roman Road at the southeast entrance to the station, there is a plaque which reads:

In memory of the 173 men, women and children
who lost their lives on the evening of
Wednesday 3rd March 1943
descending these steps to Bethnal Green
underground air raid shelter
Not forgotten.

As for Peter, he constantly saw the faces of the dead children he had to load on to the lorries. He was only short in stature and consequently was given the smaller bodies to move. He never truly recovered from this trauma and was unable to talk about it for many years. My great friend Tommy was never the same exuberant little boy and I would often find him sitting on his own deep in thought, although he would never tell me exactly what haunted him. As if the war was not traumatic enough, this one event went down as the greatest civilian disaster in the East End of London and one that is very difficult to eradicate from people's memories.

FROM GREAT

SITE OF THE WORS
OF THE SECO

IN MEM
173 MEN, WOME
WHO LOST THE
EVENING OF WEDNE
DESCENDING THESE ST
UNDERGROUND A

NOT FO

GS TO GREATER

CIVILIAN DISASTER
D WORLD WAR

ORY OF
AND CHILDREN
R LIVES ON THE
DAY 3ʳᵈ MARCH 1943
PS TO BETHNAL GREEN
R RAID SHELTER

GOTTEN

The plaque outside the southeast entrance to Bethnal Green
tube station in the East End of London.

THE BOMBING OF THE DOCKLANDS

ALTHOUGH the London docks were the constant target of the Luftwaffe bombers, amazingly they continued to cope with the flow of imports and exports that were vital to the economy of the capital. Father told me how the Germans believed that they could cripple both the industrial and commercial life of London with their constant raids, but we as a family believed differently. We knew that the workers would do everything in their power to make the docks run as smoothly as possible despite the fact that parts of the St Katharine Docks were so badly damaged that it was not possible to rebuild them. Initially the main targets were the gas works at Beckton, the Royal Arsenal factory at Woolwich and, of course, the docks. The docks weren't hard to find, the Germans simply had to follow the path of the River Thames.

Saturday, 7 September 1940, became known as Black Saturday and is one that is definitely engraved in my memory and no doubt any other East Ender who is still alive today. That day father had gone with his brother to watch West Ham play Tottenham and when he heard the drone of the plane engines overhead, West Ham were thrashing their opponents 4–1. Everyone looked to the sky and my father knew immediately it was no reconnaissance flight, they meant business. He didn't wait to see any more of the game. He rushed towards home, literally dodging bombs as they dropped no less than one hundred yards from his feet. He told me that every corner he turned, it seemed another stick bomb hit its target and people were screaming everywhere

ABOVE: The docklands ablaze after the first mass air raid on London. Tower Bridge is in the background.

as panic set in. One boy who was sitting in the barbers, only had half his hair cut as the barber ran away and left him sitting in the chair. This was the story everywhere, as people suddenly realised the German threat to attack the city had actually become a reality.

The first attack lasted for over an hour and a half and looking over towards the docklands it seemed the whole of the area was ablaze as hundreds of fires lit the sky. Once it started to get dark it was possible to see the fires from over ten miles away and because of this, the Germans were able to find their way back to attack for a second time. The night bombing lasted much longer, eight hours in fact, shaking the entire city with the deafening noise of hundreds of bombs falling one after the other. Firemen, doctors, nurses, civil defence workers, in fact everyone played a part that night in trying to save the docks and the rest of London.

My next account comes straight from the mouth of a crew member of MS *Abbekerk*, a Dutch freighter, a fast ship designed for the Holland–Australia line. The crew member in question, a Mr Finn, was a British steward who had lodged with us just prior to the Blitz. He came to visit whenever he was in the docks and had many stories to tell.

MS *Abbekerk* was docked in Albert Dock in London when the docks became the primary target for the Luftwaffe. On 7 September 1940, the *Abbekerk* was hit at about 6.00 p.m. by a bomb in the chief engineer's cabin. Directly behind the ship was a massive warehouse containing wood which went up like a tinderbox. Because of the

LEFT: Two Dornier 217 flying over the Silvertown area of London's Docklands. Fires have started near the Beckton Gasworks. West Ham greyhound track is near the centre of the picture, which was taken from a German bomber.

fire in the warehouse, the rear of the ship became excessively hot and the paint started to blister and burn. Because the crew feared that the whole ship would catch alight, the decision was made to throw any ammunition they were carrying overboard. The ammunition was under lock and key in a special store at the rear of the ship and to save time members of the crew broke the lock and quickly dumped the contents of the store into the water. As soon as they had finished the lifeboats were lowered and the crew abandoned ship, first making sure they salvaged any important papers and instruments. They rowed to the other side of the dock and waited there for instructions. As they looked out over the water, warehouses full of sugar, rum, paint and other flammables were exploding under the heat of the fire, and the river quickly became a blaze of molten liquid that poured onto the quaysides causing even more fires.

Once the fire in the warehouse was under control the crew were advised to row back to the *Abbekerk* where two tugs from the Dock Authority were waiting to tow the ship away from danger. The ship had lost power so it wasn't possible to physically move the *Abbekerk* without assistance. As the ship was moved, Finn noticed that Hold number 4 was filling up with water.

Unfortunately that was not the end of the disasters to hit the *Abbekerk*; the following day it was hit by a firebomb at about 11.00 p.m. on the rear deck. There were several oil drums on the deck which immediately caught fire and exploded. There were very few crew on board at the time as many had gone ashore, so crew members from another ship in the dock, SS *Moena*, came to help put out the fire. About an hour later, just as they had got the fire under control, another bomb exploded underneath the ship. The ship started to take in water at a great rate and began to list badly.

The following morning the master of the *Abbekerk* went to ask the dock master for help to pump out the water from his ship. Unfortunately, the dock master did not have any tugs available and had to ask the master of *Abbekerk* to wait until one became free. It wasn't until the following day that they managed to bring some pumps on board, but they were too small to cope with the amount of water and

RIGHT: A fire squad rushes along a dock wall in the East End of London to the scene of a fire.

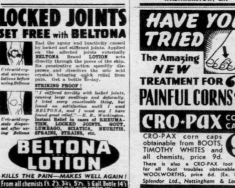
the ship slowly sank deeper and deeper into the water. The ship was eventually salvaged but it took another year and a half before it came back into active service.

MS *Abbekerk* was not the only ship to suffer, of course. Moored in Victoria Dock was the SS *Moena*, another Dutch freighter which suffered a direct hit by two bombs on 7 September at 5.30 p.m. One of the bombs exploded in the coal bunker on the port side and caused a great deal of damage. The wooden hatches of the bunker were thrown high into the air, while deck beams, steel hatches and the deck itself were severely buckled. The second bomb fell through the hatch of Hold number 5, but didn't actually explode. It did enough damage to cause the hold to flood, though. As more and more planes flew overhead, the *Moena* was hit by several firebombs, which the crew fought valiantly to keep under control. Eventually the situation became so serious that the master decided to send the majority of his crew ashore to take shelter from the incessant bombs.

Factories, warehouses and houses in the dock area were all ablaze. Several ships were on fire and in the dock itself several large barges were drifting and burning out of control, a major threat to other ships moored in the docks. One of these barges drifted dangerously close to the *Moena* and it was the quick thinking of the first and second mates who dropped the *Moena's* anchor on the barge, sinking it and quenching the fire. As the barge started to sink it sent a rain of sparks high into the sky, causing one of the warehouses close by to catch fire.

It was only the following morning that the

extent of the damage to *Moena* was fully realised. The warehouse directly next to the ship had been reduced to a pile of rubble. Aware that the Germans would return, the crews on both the *Abbekerk* and *Moena* were reduced to a bare minimum. The two ships were now moored next to each other and the skeleton crew left behind took turns to keep watch. And, as expected, the Germans did return and with renewed force. On 9 September at about 9.00 p.m. both the quay and the warehouse directly behind the ships were hit and the *Moena* was hit by several firebombs. They managed to quell the fires using buckets of sand, but the warehouse was burning so fiercely it was decided to abandon ship.

Even before the start of the Blitz, the government had known that the Port of London was going to be a major target. Unfortunately, this area was densely packed with houses and it was the poor of the East End near the docks who suffered the most. Any ships that were carrying foodstuffs were redirected to safer ports and the huge warehouses that had previously stockpiled large amounts of imported sugar, meat, dairy produce, grain and wood were emptied of much of their stock. Any provisions that were unloaded from the ships were quickly removed and taken away by either road or rail. They were strange and unforgettable sights, ones that I will never forget – especially the flocks of pigeons who just flew around all night confused by the strange light in the sky. However, out of all the disaster came a spirit that surpassed anything we had ever witnessed. A kind of endurance and courage that brought people together and helped them through the confusion and terror.

ABOVE: Admiral Evans, ARP commissioner for Greater London, watching an Auxiliary Fire Service demonstration at Surrey Commercial Docks.

ST PAUL'S CATHEDRAL

THE SECOND GREAT FIRE OF LONDON

As a born and bred Londoner it is hard for me to imagine London without the familiar dome of St Paul's Cathedral. We had enjoyed a brief respite in the bombing over the Christmas period of December 1940 and life had almost got back to normal, but we had been lulled into a false sense of security. On the night of the 29 December, the air raid sirens sounded again at about 6.00 p.m. and London was hit by the most savage attack of the Blitz. This was the night I was introduced to a weird and spine-chilling noise a bit like a muffled scream and one that I became accustomed to on successive nights. It was the sound of a bomb being launched from a great height. Within the hour there were reports that two large incendiary bombs had hit London in the region of the Guildhall off Gresham Street. Reports quickly came in of further outbreaks of fire and the local fire stations were soon being inundated with calls. Within an hour a serious fire situation had developed within the vicinity of St Paul's Cathedral, the famous Anglican cathedral that stands proudly on Ludgate Hill. At that time it was the tallest building in London, standing 111 metres (365 feet) high and I know my family feared the worst – that it would take a direct hit.

Fire was spreading quickly in the surrounding area where the buildings were old and particularly open to the risk of fire. Unfortunately, there were few roof spotters on duty that night to help stop the spread of fire, having been caught off guard after the brief break in the bombing over the holiday period. In addition to this, the owners of many of the warehouses and buildings in the area

ABOVE: St Paul's Cathedral, largely unscathed, stands behind a cleared bomb site.

had padlocked their doors for the night, which seriously hampered the firemen reaching the source of many of the smaller fires. To the south of the cathedral, cloth warehouses quickly burned to the ground. Both sides of Ludgate Hill were being ravaged by fire and many streets to the north were completely destroyed.

Although there would not normally have been a water shortage in London, the amount required to quell the fires that night, meant the fire services had to call for emergency water. However, this request took a while to put into action as pumps had to be positioned on the Thames, dockside, canals and the hose lines laid out ready to take the water. All this takes time and time was precious. As fast as was humanly possible, large river boats were put into position with their heavy pumps, and powerful lorries that were capable of laying hoses were put into action. Everything was almost in place when a report came through just before 9.00 p.m. to say that the spire of a neighbouring church was in danger of collapse any minute, endangering the Guildhall.

Every available firefighter and piece of equipment had been called out to try and stop the spread of fire which was threatening the whole city of London. The area directly around the Guildhall and St Paul's Cathedral became known as the 'danger zone' and the fire in that area was reaching alarming proportions. Fires were breaking out in literally hundreds of buildings and the sky was so bright it could almost have been a bright sunlit day. The glare from the fire could be seen far beyond the capital and every dark alleyway and narrow street was ablaze or glowing from a neighbouring fire. Firemen could be seen in almost every street, dodging fireballs, blinding sparks and thick plumes of smoke that filled the air. They never gave up, they fought on regardless of the dangers and many brave souls lost their lives that night either by falling masonry, bombs or being engulfed by flames. Even three fire stations had to be evacuated because they caught fire and the control centre had to be set up in a safer zone.

Where was I while all this was happening? Glued to the window unable to move away, I was so dumbstruck by the red glow all

RIGHT: The dome of St Paul's Cathedral on the left is shown clearly silhouetted against the glow.

around me. We had been advised to use our shelter at home as it wasn't safe to venture out on the streets that night and, although mother was aware of the danger of us being hit, she allowed Ellen and I watch knowing that we were worried about father. I remember being really scared that night, probably the most scared I had been throughout the whole period of the Blitz. It was around 10.00 p.m. when someone shouted that the roof of the Guildhall had caught fire. By now the emergency water was starting to flow and I could hear a loud cheer from the firefighters as their hoses filled with water. This meant they had a strong enough flow to stem the ferocious wall of fire. Women worked tirelessly risking their own lives as they drove through dangerous clouds of sparks and embers to bring men food to keep them going through the night. The gutters and streets ran with black water but amidst the chaos was amazing strength, courage and determination that London would not be razed to the ground.

From my viewpoint it was difficult to make out too much detail but at 12.00 I heard the all-clear and I remember my body relaxing a bit knowing that at least the bombs would stop for a while. I looked over in the direction of St Paul's Cathedral, but all I could see was an enormous pinkish-white cloud billowing upwards. As I continued to stare I could see a shape looming out of the smoke and I wasn't sure exactly what it was. Then it hit me it was the gigantic dome of St Paul's Cathedral and I yelled downstairs, 'Mum it's survived!' The dome stood there proudly gradually getting clearer and clearer; to me it was like a miracle and I knew from that moment that my father would be OK.

RIGHT: St Paul's Cathedral after a direct hit during the Blitz in London .

When father arrived home in the early hours exhausted and black, he sat down in the scullery and told us about the great fires of London while he drank his strong, sweet mug of tea. He said that many of the buildings around the cathedral had been burned to the ground, but thanks to a group of amazing volunteers called St Paul's Watch, the cathedral itself had been saved. They took it upon themselves to douse incendiary bombs as soon as they fell which prevented fires taking hold in the cathedral itself. It didn't come out completely unscathed as a bomb demolished the High Altar completely and the Crypt suffered minor damage, but that was nothing compared to the rest of London. One of the volunteers was standing inside the cathedral and he told my father that the light coming through the stained glass windows was amazing, little did he know that would be the last time he, or indeed anyone else, would see those windows because shortly afterwards they were shattered sending bright shards of glass across the cathedral floor.

St Paul's Cathedral became a symbol of Britain's undefeatable spirit and I do believe that night it made our nation even more determined to overcome the enemy. Father told us that even our prime minister, Winston Churchill, had seen the survival of the building as a morale booster, saying, 'At all costs, St Paul's must be saved!' Of course his wish came true and I know that I felt stronger after that night – to me the cathedral symbolised hope. If a building of that stature can survive twenty-eight bombs then we as a nation must be invincible!

ABOVE: Aerial view of London, including St. Paul's Cathedral, after the Blitz.

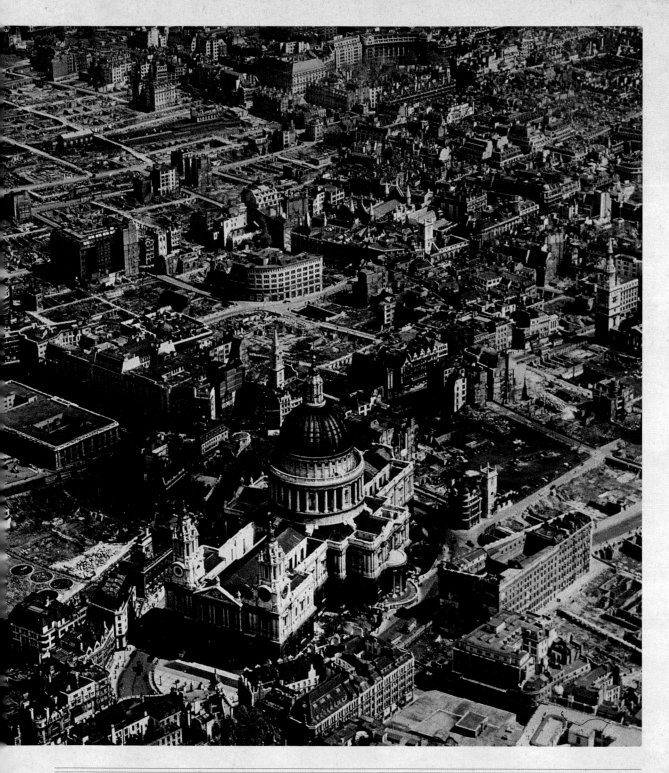

THE DAY
I MET
CHURCHILL

WINSTON Churchill became prime minister on 10 May 1940 and, to us and many other families, he quickly became our hero and our hope that the war would soon be over. Instead of fleeing to a place of safety, Churchill remained in London throughout the Blitz along with those who suffered. He was against Nazism and all it stood for and his regular morale-boosting speeches on the radio did much to allay people's fears. I remember, even as a small child, listening avidly to the radio after the blackout curfew even though many of his big words went straight over my head. Father said that as long as we had a figurehead like Churchill we would never lose the war and, of course, I believed him. I revered this man who seemed to constantly have a cigar hanging from the corner of his mouth and wondered whether he ever removed his hat. When father told me he was coming to the East End of London to see the damage, you can imagine my excitement. To me it would be like meeting the queen. Mother said I shouldn't get my hopes up and that in all possibility I would never actually get to see him. Still, on 8 September, I put on my very best dress and mother helped me pick some flowers from the top of the Anderson shelter which she tied with one of my hair ribbons in a neat bow.

Accompanied by mother and Ellen, we left the house around 11.00 a.m. and started to work our way along the streets towards the docks. This was the area that had been hardest hit the previous night and we knew that Churchill wanted to see the damage for himself. It was quite slow progress as we had to pick our way carefully

LEFT: British prime minister, Winston Churchill, gives the famous v-sign for victory on the steps of Number 10 Downing Street.

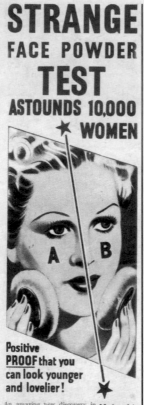

through rubble, and scary as we had not realised just how many houses had been destroyed in the night. For the kids who lived around the docks they must have had to live with the taste of dirt on their lips and the smell of burning in their nostrils twenty-four hours a day. Many of the houses had been sealed off with boards up against their windows and doors, I imagine to keep the children from playing in the rubble. I vividly remember the crunch of broken glass underfoot and the leafless trees in the gardens as if winter had come too early. Another smell, something I had not experienced before, was that of sap where all the bark had been stripped from the trees in gardens and parks where children used to play.

I remember seeing one house that looked as though it had been cut in half with a giant knife. The upstairs floor jutted out from the rest of the building as if it was suspended in mid-air. Amazingly, there was still a bed, a mattress and a wardrobe standing untouched with the curtains from the broken window flapping alarmingly in the breeze. I remember thinking it looked like a giant dolls' house and felt quite distressed when I

saw some poor child's doll lying on the pavement covered with shards of glass.

Everywhere were piles of furniture that had been either blown out of the houses or simply thrown out of the damaged buildings. These once loved pieces were now covered with glass, dust, water stains and soot. It made me realise just how lethal the bombs were that Hitler was dropping on our London and I think I said a little prayer as I walked along asking that my family and house could remain safe. Everyone was affected by the terrible period of the Blitz, even the king and queen narrowly missed death when two bombs exploded in a courtyard at Buckingham Palace while they were in residence. They, like Churchill, refused to desert their people and decided to stay and face the danger, although they did send their children to Windsor Castle to be away from the constant bombardment. Also, like Churchill, they made regular visits to bomb sites and munitions factories, but unfortunately I never got to meet them. Anyway, back to my original story of meeting Churchill.

We knew we must be getting close to where Churchill would

RIGHT: King George VI and Queen Elizabeth (later the Queen Mother) inspecting the bomb damage to Buckingham Palace after a heavy Nazi air raid.

be stopping as there was quite a crowd of people gathered, all chatting excitedly. We asked someone if the prime minister had arrived yet, and the woman smiled and told us that we hadn't missed anything. I was relieved and suddenly remembered the bunch of flowers I had been carrying. I looked down to see they had wilted and looked rather sad; this was because I had unknowingly been clutching them rather too tightly as we walked through the sad-looking streets of the docks. However sad and dejected they looked, I was not prepared to discard my bouquet, this was a gift I intended to hand directly to the great man. Mother told me to find somewhere to sit as we might have to wait a long time. In her pocket she carried a few barley sugars and she handed me one and told me to 'make it last'. I sat down on top of a pile of bricks and waited making up stories of what I would say to Churchill when he arrived.

We didn't have to wait too long, about thirty-five minutes I would guess, before a cheer went up and a party of six men walked towards the crowd. Right in the centre was the man himself.

'He's here, he's here,' mum shouted to me. Although in truth I didn't need telling because I was already jumping to my feet, straining to see if I could catch sight of him. I stood on tippy toes but I still couldn't see over or through the crowd of people. Desperate to catch one small glimpse of this famous man I pushed my way between the bodies, ignoring the rude remarks from several of the women as I went. Eventually I was near the front and I could make out Churchill's legs quite clearly. I knew they were his because he had a

ABOVE: Huge crowds followed Winston Churchill when he inspected damage and bomb craters in London.

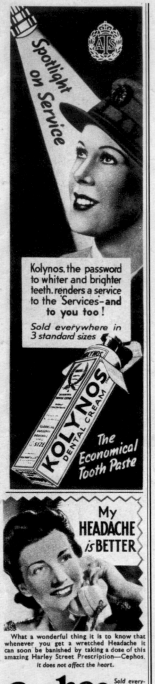

neatly ironed crease down the front of his trousers and his shoes, which would have been highly polished when he started out, were now stained with grey and red dust.

'Mr Churchill, Mr Churchill,' I called as I made my way past the last obstruction of bodies. At first he didn't hear me over the cheering. I tried again and this time he turned in my direction. My stomach did a somersault and for one horrible moment I thought I was going to be sick right on the spot. However, I did manage to gain my composure, well as much as an eleven-year-old child can do, and ran out from the crowd and curtsied right in front of my hero.

'We think you're great, sir,' I said in my very best voice – not the one I used to play with Tommy but more like the polished voices I heard on the radio. 'Will you please accept my flowers, 'cos I want to give yer something?' forgetting all about the fact that I was supposed to be talking 'posh'.

To my complete surprise, the man himself bent down until his face was level with my own and said, 'Thank you so much I would love to accept your gift. And what is your name?'

For a moment I was too overcome to speak, but eventually managed to stammer out my name … 'M-m-m-ary, sir. M-mary Hanway, sir'.

'Thank you Mary Hanway,' he replied and shook my hand. Then he walked away down the street and continued his inspection of the damage.

'I can't believe you did that,' Ellen said running up to me.

'Well I did, and I don't think I will ever wash my hand again. 'E touched me you know!' I said still not quite believing what had happened.

That was without doubt the best day of the entire Blitz. I had managed to be a minute fragment of Churchill's extraordinary life and for me that became the turning point of the war, from that moment I knew my family would survive. And I wasn't wrong.

Walking home after the event I was talking excitedly to mother and Ellen and saying how wonderful Churchill was and kept going on and on about the fact that he had shook my hand until they must have been sick of the sound of my voice. I then had a strange feeling that we were being followed and as I looked behind me, a pathetic looking mongrel dog was trailing behind me with his tail tucked between his legs, his ears flat against his head which he carried very low almost touching the ground. There was blood trickling down a wound on his shoulder and his whole body was covered with dust. Mother warned me not to touch him in case he bit me, but I knew he wouldn't bite, I knew he wanted comfort. He wore no collar to say where he had come from or what he was called, and as I got closer he whimpered and licked my hand. I stroked his head and gave him my one last barley sugar, which he ate so quickly I knew he must be starving. It took some persuading to allow him to come home with us, but luckily my mother was a sucker for animals and agreed we could take him home and give him something to eat. Ellen wasn't nearly so easy to convince I think she thought the mangy mutt, as she called him, would not do her reputation any good.

The dog became known as 'Winston' and except when I was at school, he never left my side. After a bath and a bit of delousing, he was allowed to sleep on the end of my bed and even today it brings a tear to my eye to remember probably one of the best friends I ever had.

ABOVE: Churchill touring the Blitz damaged streets in the City of London.

PICKING UP

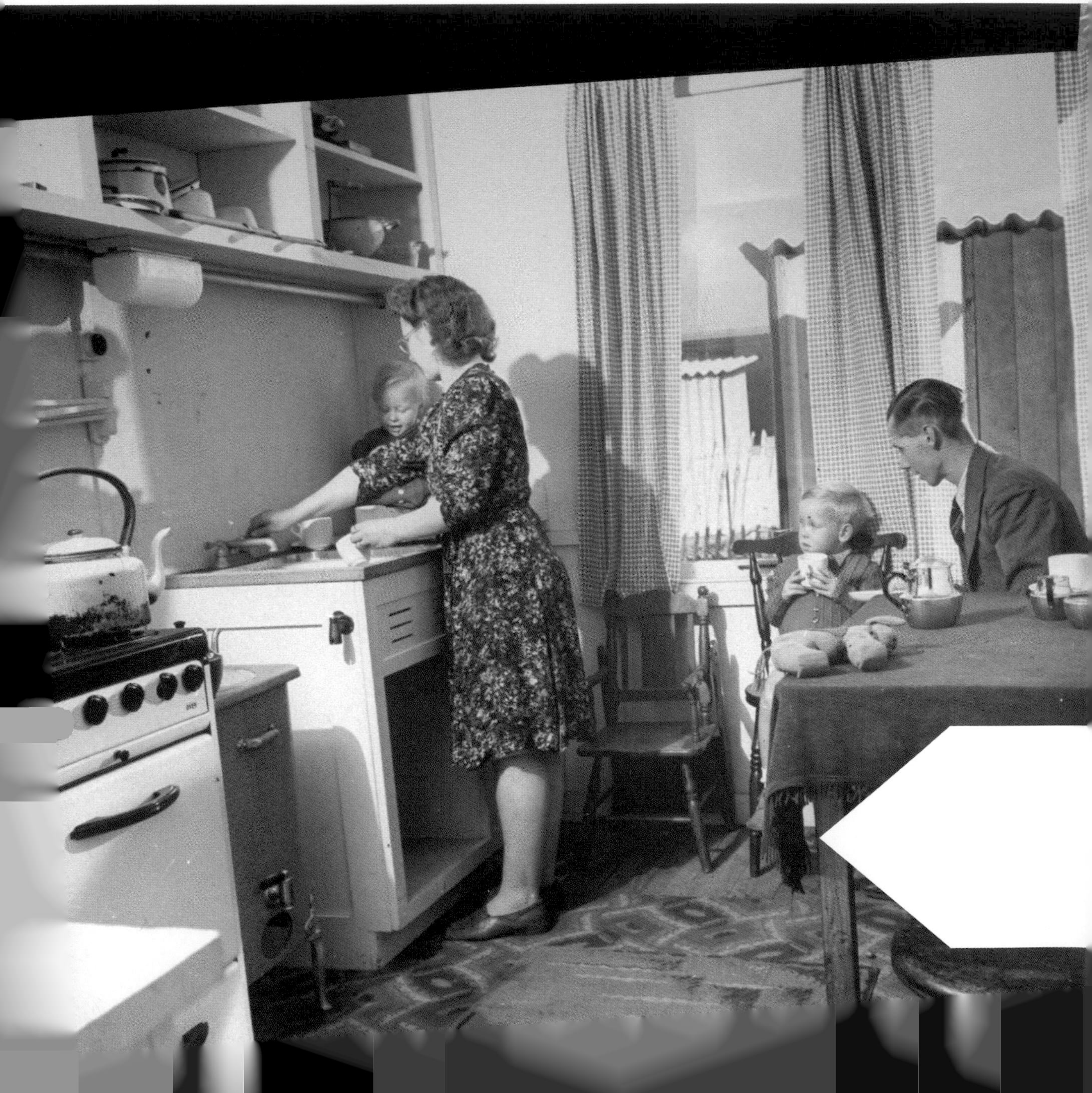

THE PIECES

THE last night of the Blitz, and probably the worst for us Londoners, was 10 May 1941. On that night we were sheltering in our Anderson shelter and the noise of the planes and the bombs never seemed to end. That night more than five hundred planes and seven hundred tons of high explosives pummelled the city. We were all scared and that was the night I really didn't think we were going to survive. Morning came, all went quiet, and then we heard that the human cost of that one single raid was nearly 1,500 people killed and another 1,800 seriously wounded. I didn't usually cry, but I did cry that morning, mainly because mother and Ellen were crying as there seemed no end to Hitler's punishment of the British people.

We expected the same the next night, but nothing happened, nor the night after and we saw a glimmer of hope. I asked my father why they had stopped bombing and he told me that Hitler needed his army to fight the Russians now, so the raids on London ceased. Of course that wasn't the end of the war, but it was the end of the night after night bombing raids to try and obliterate our capital.

RIGHT: A Soviet poster depicting the alliance between Great Britain and the Soviet Union against Germany.

ВСТРЕЧА НАД БЕРЛИНОМ

НАЗНАЧИЛИ НАРОДЫ-БРАТЬЯ
НАД ВРАЖЬИМ ГОРОДОМ СВИДАНИЕ.
ОТ ЭТОГО РУКОПОЖАТЬЯ
НЕ ПОЗДОРОВИТСЯ ГЕРМАНИИ!

ХУД. КУКРЫНИКСЫ   ТЕМА- Н. ВИВШИЦ   ТЕКСТ С. МАРШАК

БЕРЛИН

(TRANSLATION) **MEETING OVER BERLIN**
THE BROTHER-NATIONS ARRANGED
A RENDEZVOUS OVER THE ENEMY'S TOWN.
THIS HANDSHAKE WILL NOT BE HEALTHY FOR THE GERMANS

Artist: KUKRINIKSY.   Theme by I. LIVSHITZ.   Words by S. MARSHAK.

It was estimated that by the time the Blitz was over around 16,000 people had been killed and 180,000 wounded. One in six Londoners had been rendered homeless and the aftermath of the destruction had ever-lasting effects. Of course the end of the Blitz did not mean the end of the war, but to a little girl a new lightness came over me and I began to feel a sense of well-being. We still had occasional raids which lasted for the next three years and Hitler's new bigger and more powerful weapons presented a new threat to Londoners, but at least it was not every single night and people could get back to some kind of normality.

As I have said before, the East End was hit the hardest, particularly because many of the houses were already in a poor condition and could not withstand the constant bombardment. Over forty per cent of the houses in Stepney were destroyed and near the docks as high as eight-five per cent. That is a lot of people left without any homes and belongings. Of course the government could not have forecast the level of homelessness that would be caused by the Blitz and provisions were totally inadequate. People relied totally on friends and relatives to help them out and we converted our back parlour into a bedroom so that at

THIS IS AN ACTUAL FLYING BOMB

BALLOON ARMAMENT

LEFT: East Londoners are made homeless during German air raids on London.
ABOVE: A V1 flying bomb, or Doodlebug, on show at Roote's, Piccadilly, London.

least one family would have a place to sleep. With their ration books we managed to get enough supplies to feed us all. I wouldn't say that we ate well, but we survived.

There were rest centres set up for homeless people, but they could not cope with the vast numbers. Workers were deployed to make good any homes that could be salvaged and by August 1941 over one million houses had been made at least weatherproof. It wasn't luxury by any means, but it was a roof over people's heads and for that they were extremely grateful. The process of rebuilding was slow and many people had to live in temporary huts on sites where houses had been destroyed by bombs or fire.

As the mammoth task of clearing sites got underway, it opened up a whole can of worms. Gas mains were badly damaged, but because many of the original plans had been destroyed essential repairs were severely hampered. There wasn't a part of London that hadn't been affected by the Blitz. Factories, hospitals, schools, railways, churches and shops were all hit and every able body was asked to muck in and help with rebuilding what was left. Even school children were asked to help fill in bomb craters and sift through rubble for anything that was still in one piece.

Shopping was very difficult because so many shops had been destroyed. This meant that provisions were in short supply and what provisions were left had to be sold out of makeshift structures. Everyone was determined though and many shopkeepers put up large signs telling Hitler 'WE ARE NOT BEATEN!'

ABOVE: A construction crew works on completing demolition on a site largely destroyed in an air raid.

In 1944, Winston Churchill introduced his 'Temporary Housing Programme', which was aimed at providing large numbers of houses quickly and cheaply for families who had been crippled by the war. These houses became known as prefabricated or prefabs for short. They were made in factories and then taken bit by bit to the site and assembled there – a triumph in design and a much-needed answer for those people without homes. Tommy and his family were rehoused in one of these prefabs and of course I was a regular visitor. In fact I was quite jealous of his posh new home with its two bedrooms, living room, fitted kitchen, hallway and hot and cold running water. They also had a gas cooker in the kitchen, a built-in refrierator and a fitted bathroom with a heated towel rail. These were real luxuries and not ones that we enjoyed in our semi.

The docks, which had been so badly hit during the Blitz, took years to rebuild and business did not return to normal until the mid-1950s. Parts of St Katharine Docks could not be rebuilt and the East India Export Dock had to be filled in because it was beyond repair.

There is no doubt that the war bought out the best in people, everyone rallied regardless of their circumstances. It was hard for those people who lost loved ones and even harder if a body could not be found or identified, because it meant there was no funeral, no closing ceremony and I know my aunt suffered because of this, losing her only son to war. Everyone knew someone who had been killed or injured, but most people put on a brave face and carried on as best they could. They were tough times, scary times, but good times and ones I can only look back on with a mixture of horror and delight. As a child I was probably shielded from the worst of the war, but I know from the look on my father's face after a night of fighting fires that it was one of the most difficult times that Londoners have ever had to face.

My last memory I wish to share with you was when mother decided to take me on a shopping trip to Woolworths in Deptford. We had been told they had some new stock delivered and I was going to be treated to something for passing an exam at school. We got on the bus, but when we got close to Deptford we were told the bus could go no further.

'What's happened?' mother asked the conductor.

'There's been a bomb in New Cross Road and apparently a lot of people have been killed,' he told us.

The reality was that one hundred and sixty people lost their lives that day and my favourite store, Woolworths, was nothing but a pile of rubble.

I never did get my surprise, but then that is what war does to people, it destroys any kind of normality. I am thankful I survived the Blitz and that I am able to share my memories, because I met so many wonderful people during those months that their memory will always be engraved in my heart.

LEFT: People were not used to the luxuries afforded them by the new fitted kitchens inside the prefabricated bungalows – an electric oven, hot running water and a fridge.

Picture Credits
The publisher would like to thank the following for permission to reproduce photographs:
Cover: Composite © John Eder & Anthony Prudente / **Internal:** 8, 12, 38, 67, 68, 86, 116, 123 © Time & Life Pictures/ Getty Images / 10, 11, 16, 17, 18, 19, 20, 25, 26, 29, 30, 32, 33, 34, 37, 40, 44, 46, 50, 52, 56, 58, 59, 60, 63, 71, 72, 81, 89, 90, 93, 95, 103, 105, 106, 113, 115, 117, 119, 120, 121 © Getty Images / 14, 48, 74, 106, 108, 111, 124 © Popperfoto/Getty Images / 16, 23, 43, 49, 98, 101 © SSPL via Getty Images / 79 © Anthony Haigh / Alamy / 84 © Anthony Prudente.

ISBN: 978-0-9561428-5-6

Canary Press
An imprint of Omnipress Ltd
Chantry House, 22 Upperton Road
Eastbourne, East Sussex BN21 1BF
England

Printed and bound in Italy

10 9 8 7 6 5 4 3 2 1

Editor: Vivian Foster
Production Manager: Benita Estevez
Cover and internal design: Anthony Prudente